AN INTRODUCTION TO TABLETS

LADI ALIK KUMAR

To My Friend Dolly, My Mother and My Father without whom this
book would have been completed earlier...

Contents

Foreword

Everyday there will be a new challenge to us for facing. The main aim of the book is to create a clear concept on tablets. Generally in each day of our academic life we are receivnig diffirent types of questions related to pharma profession like tablets , capsules etc. and we also confused to answer. So overcoming these all things is a major issue where we will clear these things by covering this book.

Acknowledgements

Dedicated to all those people who helped me to write the book.
THNAK YOU

CHAPTER ONE

TABLETS

Introduction

USP defines a Tablet as a solid dosage form containing medicaments with or without excipients.

The Indian Pharmacopoeia defines pharmaceutical tablets as solid, hard, flat, or biconvex dishes, containing a single dose of a drug or mixture of drugs, with or without diluents.

Advantages of Tablet over other Oral drug delivery systems from Patients view:

- They are easy to swallow, carry and have a pleasing appearance.
- Sugar coating can mask unpleasant taste, and dosage does not need to be measured.
- Tablets are divided into halves and quarters during manufacture. This makes it easier to break a fractional dose whenever it is needed.

From Manufacturer View:

- It is possible to incorporate a precise amount of medication, even if it is very small.
- The tablet provides the best combination of chemical, mechanical, and microbiological stability of all oral dosage forms.
- Due to their mass production, their production cost is relatively low, making them economical.
- They are generally the cheapest and easiest to package and ship of all oral dosage forms.
- There are some specialized tablets that are prepared for modified release profiles of the drug. Identification of products with embossed or monogrammed punch faces is the easiest and most cost-effective method as it requires no additional processing steps.

Disadvantages of tablet dosage form

- Children and unconscious patients may have difficulty swallowing it.
- It may be challenging to formulate or manufacture a tablet that provides adequate or full bioavailability for drugs whose wetting and dissolution properties are poor, as well as high absorption in the gastrointestinal tract.
- Encapsulation or coating is required for bitter testing drugs, substances with objectionable odors, or substances able to withstand oxygen. In such cases, capsules may offer the best and lowest cost.

- Some drugs are resistant to compression into dense compacts because of their amorphous nature and low density character.

CHAPTER TWO

TYPES OF TABLETS

Tablets are classified into following types

Types of tablets-

a. <u>**Tablets Ingested Orally:**</u>

- Compressed tablets
- Multiple compressed tablets
- Enteric coated tablets
- Sugar coated tablets
- Film coated tablets
- Chewable tablets

b. <u>**Tablets used in the oral cavities:**</u>

- Buccal Tablets
- Sublingual tablets
- Lozenges
- Dental cones

c. <u>**Tablets administered by other routes:**</u>

- ○ Implantation tablets
- ○ Vaginal tablets

d. **<u>Tablets used to prepare solutions:</u>**

- ○ Effervescent tablets
- ○ Dispensing tablets
- ○ Hypodermic tablets
- ○ Tablet triturates

A. Tablets ingested orally-

Compressed tablets:-

- There is no special coating needed on these tablets since they are formed by compression. Generally, they consist of powders, crystals, or grains, either alone or with other excipients.
- Tablets containing water-soluble drugs dissolve in the stomach after swallowing and are absorbed in the gastrointestinal tract and distributed throughout the body.

E.g. Paracetamol tablets.

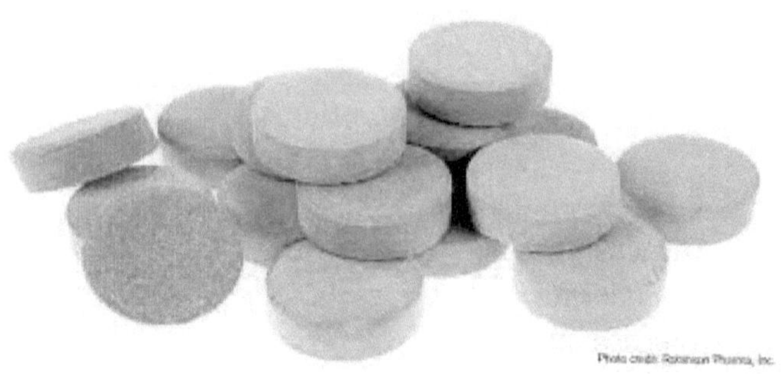

Compressed Tablet

Multiple Compressed tablets / Layered tablets-

- These are compressed tablets that have been compressed more than once. A previously compressed tablet granulation is compressed on top of the additional tablet granulation to produce such tablets. Two or three layers of tablets may be made by repeating the operation.

- For incompatibility prevention, the ingredients of the formulation except the incompatible substance are compressed into a tablet, and then the incompatible substance along with the necessary excipients are compressed over the tablet.

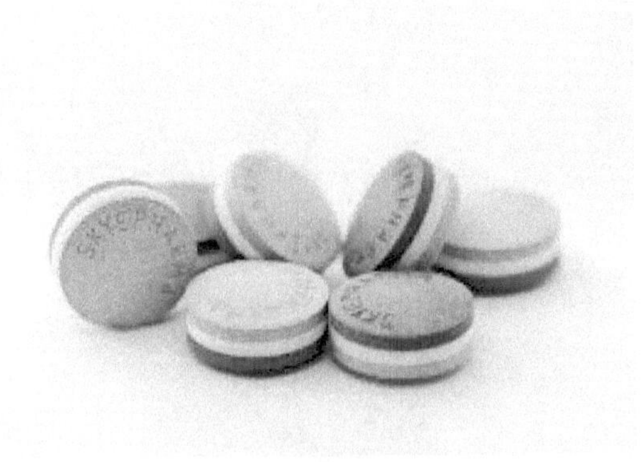

Multiple Compressed Tablet

Enteric coated tablets:

- It is a compressed tablet designed to bypass the stomach and dissolve only in the intestine once swallowed.
- A coating of cellulose acetate phthalate (CAP) provides resistance to the acidic pH of the gastric fluid, but gets disintegrated when it comes into contact with the alkaline pH of the intestine.

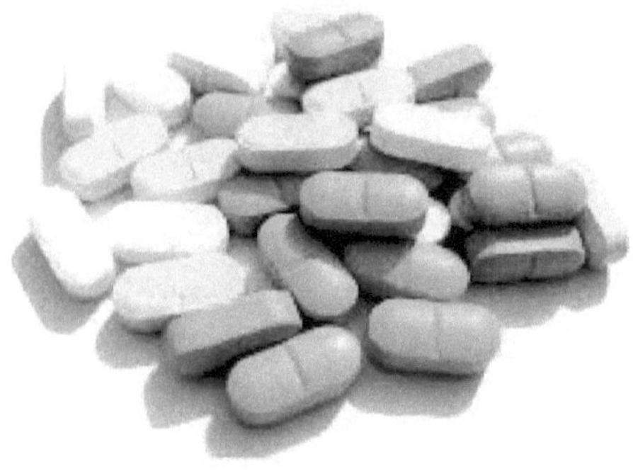

Enteric Coated Tablets

Sugar coated tablets:

- The tablets are compressed and coated with sugar. The purpose of these coatings is to mask the bitter taste and unpleasant odour of the medication. The sugar coating protects the drug from atmospheric effects as well as making the tablet elegant.

SUGAR COATED TABLETS

Sustained action tablets:

- After oral administration, these tablets release the drug at a predetermined time and prolong the duration of the medication's effect. The orally administered tablets release the medication in a sufficient quantity when required in order to maintain a maximal concentration of the drug in the blood at all times.

E.g. Diclofenac SR tablets.

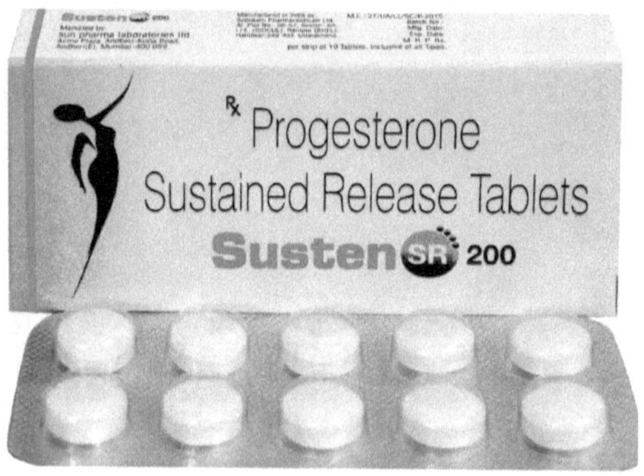

SUSTAINED RELEASE TABLET

Film coated tablets:

- The compressed tablets having a film coating of some polymer substance, such as hydroxy propyl cellulose, hydroxy propyl methyl cellulose and ethyl cellulose.
- By coating the medicament with a film, it is protected from atmoshphere effects. Sugar coated tablets are usually more elegant and have a better taste than film coated tablets.

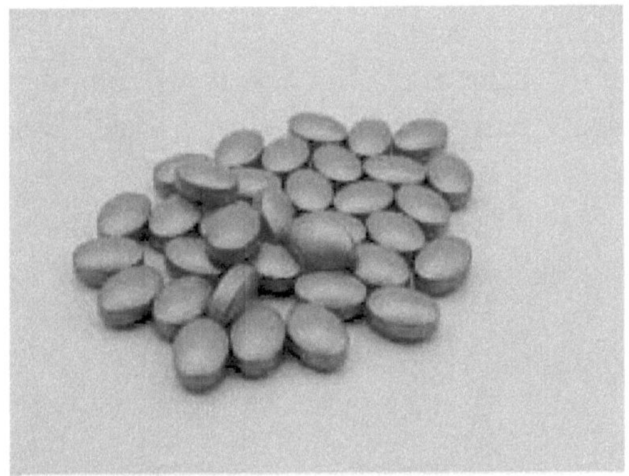

FILM COATED TABLET

Chewable tablets:

- These tablets must be broken and chewed between the teeth before ingestion. Those with difficulty swallowing and those who dislike swallowing can take these tablets.
- The taste and flavor of these tablets should be very acceptable.

Ex- Antacid tablets (Digiene).

B. Tablets used in the oral cavities –

Buccal tablets:

- The tablets should be placed in the buccal pouch of the cheek, where they disintegrate or erode slowly and are absorbed directly in the buccal cavity without entering the alimentary canal.

- Therefore, they are formulated and compressed with sufficient pressure to give a h ard tablets. e.g. Progesterone tablets.

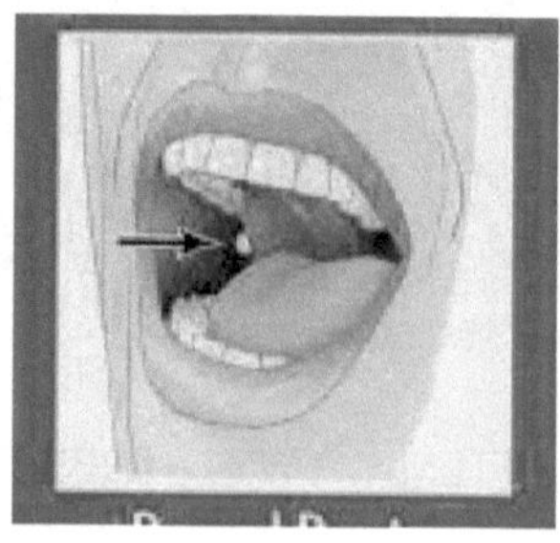

BUCCAL TABLET

Sublingual tablets:

The tablets dissolve or disintegrate quickly under the tongue and are absorbed directly without passing through the GIT. E.g. tablets of nitroglycerin, isoproterenol hydrochloride or erythrityl tetranitrate

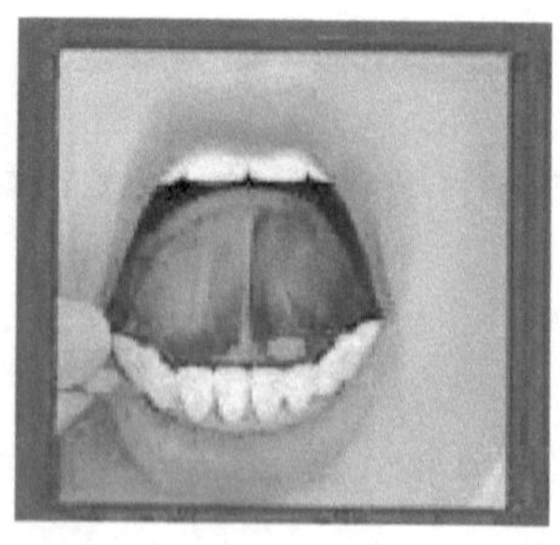

SUBLINGUAL TABLET

Lozenges tablets:

- These tablets are designed to exert a local effect in the mouth or throat. These tablets are commonly used as a treatment for sore throats and to control coughs associated with common colds. The preparations may also contain local anesthetics, antibiotics, antibacterial agents, and astringents.
- They are prepared by compression at high pressure and usually contain a sweetener, flavouring agent, and a substance that imparts a cooling effect. E.g. Vicks lozenges, Strepsils.

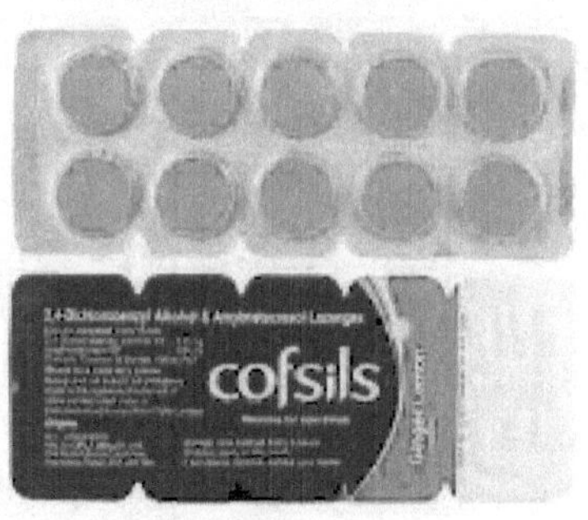

LOZENGES

Dental cones:

- These compressed tablets are meant for placing in tooth sockets after tooth extraction. A slow-release antibacterial compound or an astringent are used to reduce bleeding following such extraction and prevent bacteria from multiplying.
- These tablets contain lactose, sodium bicarbonate, and sodium chloride as excipients. It usually takes 20 to 40 minutes for these cones to dissolve.

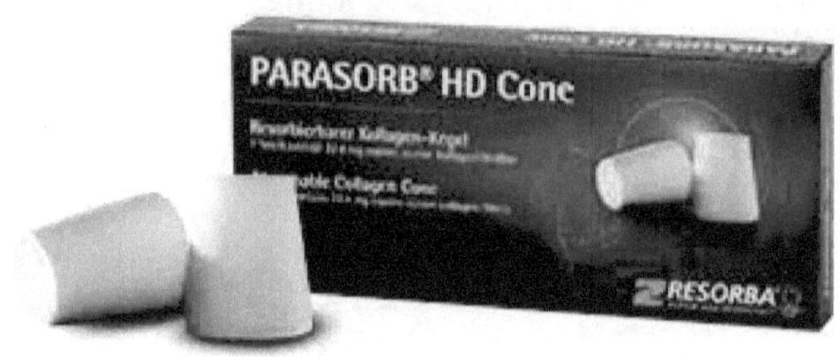

DENTAL CONES

C. Tablets administered by other routes:
Implantation Tablets:

- The tablets are inserted subcutaneously or under the skin following a minor surgery. They are then slowly absorbed. Typically, these are made by fusion, but heavy compression is also possible. Each implant must be packed individually in sterile condition and must be sterile. hormones such as testosterone steroids for contraception.A major function of implants is to administer hormones such as testosterone steroids for contraception. Birth control tablets are very useful for this purpose.

- Implant tablets have several disadvantages, including administration, changing release rate with surface area changes, and the possibility of tissue reactions.

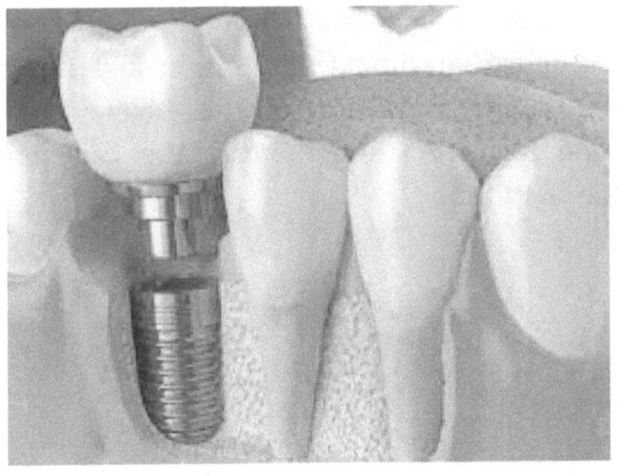

IMPLANTS

Vaginal tablets:

- These tablets are meant to dissolve slowly in the vaginal cavity. The tablets are typically ovoid or pear shaped for the ease of insertion. these tablets are used to release steroids or antimicrobial agents. the tablets are often buffered to promote a pH favorable to the action of a specified antimicrobial agent. The contains easily soluble components like lactose or sodium bicarbonate.

D. Tablets used to prepare solutions: Effervescent tablets:

- These tablets along with the active medicament contain ingredients like sodium bicarbonate, citric acid and tartaric acid which react in the presence of water liberating carbon dioxide and producing effervescence leading to disintegration of the tablet, thus fastens solution formation and increase the palatability. Eg. Histac (Ranitidine)

EFFERVESCENT TABLETS

Dispensing tablets:

- These tablets provide a convenient quantity of potent drug that can be easily converted into powder and incorporated into liquids, which eliminates the need to weigh small quantities. It is recommended that these tablets never be dispensed as a dosage form. They are only provided as a convenience for extemporaneous compounding.
- The drugs commonly used are mild silver potentiate, merbromin bichloride, and quarternary ammonium compounds.

Hypodermic tablets:

- Hypodermic tablets are soft, readily soluble tablets that were originally used to prepare injected solutions. It is administered parenterally by dissolving these tablets in sterile water or injectable water. Since the resulting solution is not always sterile, these tablets are not preferred nowadays.

HYPODERMIC TABLETS

Tablet triturates (Moulded tablets):

- These are powders that have been molded into tablets. It is typically a flat, circular disc with a potent substance mixed with lactose, lactose and sucrose, dextrose, or some other suitable diluent.
- The addition of water-insoluble additives is avoided as they are intended to disintegrate rapidly in the presence of moisture. It is appropriate to call them 'tablet triturate' because they usually contain triturations (trituration = dilution with an inert substance).

TABLET TRITURATE MOULD

CHAPTER THREE

TABLET INGREDIENTS

In addition to active ingredients, tablet contains a number of inert materials known as additives or excipients. Different excipients are:

1. Diluent / Filler
2. Binder and adhesive
3. Disintegrants
4. Lubricants and glidants
5. Colouring agents
6. Flavoring agents and Sweetening agents

Function of excipients-

- Impart weight, accuracy, & volume.
- Improve solubility
- Increase stability
- Enhance bioavailability
- Modifying drug release
- Assist product identification
- Increase patient acceptability
- Facilitate dosage form design

1. DILUENTS

The diluents used in tablet formulations are used to increase the bulk of the tablets when the drug dosage themselves is not enough to achieve it.

It may also be to provide better tablet properties such as better cohesion, to facilitate direct compression manufacturing, or to improve flow.

A diluent should have following properties:

1. They must be non-toxic and low cost.
2. They must be commercially available in acceptable grade
3. They must be physiologically inert, physically & chemically stable by themselves & in combination with the drugs.
4. They must be free from all microbial contamination.
5. They do not alter the bioavailability of drug.
6. They must be color compatible.

Characteristics of an ideal diluents

- They must be nontoxic and acceptable to the regulatory agencies in all countries where the product is to be marketed.
- They must be commercially available in an acceptable grade in all countries where the product is to be manufactured.

- They must be cheap compared to the active ingredients and must be physiologically inert.
- They must be chemically stable alone and/or in combination with the drug(s) and/or other tablet components.
- They must be color-compatible (should not produce any off-color appearance).
- They must have no negative effects on the bioavailability of the drug(s) in the product

Commonly used tablet diluents-

1. 1- Lactose-anhydrous and spray dried lactose
2. Directly compressed starch-Sta Rx 1500
3. Hydrolyzed starch-Emdex and Celutab
4. Microcrystalline cellulose-Avicel (PH 101and PH 102)
5. Dibasic calcium phosphate dehydrate
6. Calcium sulphate dihydrate
7. Mannitol and Sorbitol
8. Sucrose- Sugartab, DiPac, Nutab
9. Dextrose

Lactose

In tablet formulation, lactose is the most commonly used diluent. Anhydrous and hydrous forms are available. Moisture can be absorbed by anhydrous forms when exposed to high humidity. A moisture proof package or container should be used for such tablets. It is generally recommended that the hydrous form of lactose be used when wet granulation is employed.

- Two grades of lactoses are commercially available:

i. A 60 to 80 mesh – coarse
ii. a 80 to 100 mesh – regular grade

<u>Advantages</u>:

• Almost all drugs, whether hydrous or anhydrous, have no reaction with lactose.

• A good release rate is shown by lactose formulations. Its granulations are easily dried, and the disintegration time of lactose tablets is not greatly affected by tablet hardness.

• <u>Disadvantages</u>:

• Lactose reacts with amine drug bases in presence of alkaline lubricants e.g. metal stearates (e.g. magnesium stearate) and gradually discolours (dark brown) with time due to the formation of furaldehyde. This reaction is called <u>Maillard reaction</u>.

The diluent has a low cost.

Calcium salts ((DCP/TCP)

Dibasic calcium phosphate dihydrate (or dicalcium orthophosphate) (DCP) [$CaHPO_4, 2 H_2O$], Calcium sulfate dihydrate ($CaSO_4 , 2H_2O$).

<u>Advantages</u>:

These diluents exist in their commonly salt form as hydrates and contain significant amounts of bound water. Calcium sulfate's bound water is not released below 800°C. The amount of unbound moisture in them is very low. As a result, these

Water-sensitive drugs can be diluted with salts. The diluent is superior to anhydrous diluent, which has a moderate to high moisture requirement.

Disadvantages:

• Tetracycline products made with calcium phosphate diluent had less than half the bioavailability of the standard product. Divalent cation (Ca^{++}) form insoluble complexes and salts with number of amphoteric or acidic functionality antibiotics, which generally reduces their absorption (*which is also why milk should not be co- administered with these drug*).

Spray dried lactose

<u>Advantages:</u>

• It is used for direct compression (containing drug + diluent + disintegrant + lubricant). In addition to the direct compression properties, spray dried lactose also has good flow characteristics. It can usually be combined with as much as 20 to 25% of active ingredients without losing these advantageous features.

Disadvantages:

• If spray dried lactose is allowed to dry out and the moisture content falls below the usual 3% level, the material loses some of its direct compressional characteristics.
• Spray-dried lactose is especially prone to darkening in the presence of excess moisture, amines, and other compounds owing to Maillard reactions. Hence, a neutral or acid lubricant should be used.

Starch

- Starch may be obtained from corn, wheat or potatoes and rice. It is occasionally used as a tablet diluent. USP grade of starch is usually possesses moisture content between 11 to 14%.
- Specially dried types of starch that have a standard moisture level of 2-4% are available, but are costly. Use of such starches in wet granulation is wasteful since their moisture level increase to 6-8% following moisture exposure.

Directly compressible starches

- **Sta–Rx 1500–** free flowing, directly compressible starch. It is used as diluent, binder, disintegrant.
- **Emdex and Celutab** – are two hydrolyzed starches – contains dextrose 90–92% and maltose 3–5%
- free flowing and directly compressible and may be used in place or mannitol in chewable tablets because of their sweetness and smooth feeling in the mouth.

Dextrose (D–Glucose)

- Available in two forms: as hydrates and anhydrous forms.

- Dextrose may sometimes be combined in formulation to replace some of the spray- dried lactose, which may reduce the tendency of the resulting tablets to darken.

Mannitol

Advantages

- Because of the negative heat of solution (cooling sensation in the mouth) its slow solubility, and its pleasant feeling in the mouth, it is widely used in chewable tablets.
- It is relatively non-hygroscopic and can be used in vitamin formulations.
- Low calorie content and non-carcinogenic.

Disadvantages

- Costly and has poor flow characteristics and usually require fairly high lubricant level.

Sorbitol

- It is an optical isomer of mannitol and is sometimes combined with mannitol formulations to reduce the diluent cost.
- Disadvantages:- It is hygroscopic at humidities above 65%.

Sucrose

- Some sucrose based diluents are:
- **Sugar tab**– 90 to 93% sucrose + 7 to 10% invert sugar
- **Di Pac** – 97% sucrose + 3% modified dextrins
- **Nu Tab**– 95% sucrose + 4% invert sugar + small amount of corn starch + Mg-stearate <u>Advantages:</u> They are all used for direct compression.

<u>Disadvantages:</u> All are hygroscopic when exposed to elevated humidity.

Microcrystalline cellulose (MCC)

- Trade Name : Avicel – is a directly compression material

Two grades are available PH 101 ? powder PH 102? granules

<u>Advantages:</u>

1. It acts as diluent and disintegrating agents.

2. Binders and Adhesive

A binder or granulator is an agent that provides cohesive properties to powdered materials

2. BINDERS AND ADHESIVES

A binder or granulator is an agent that provides cohesive properties to powdered materials

<u>Objective of incorporating binders</u>

• They impart a cohesiveness to the tablet formulation (both direct compression and wet– granulation method)

which insures the tablet remaining intact after compression.

• They improves the free-flowing qualities by the formation of granules of desired size and hardness.

Characteristics of binder

Method-I

- ○ Binders are used in dry form in the powder and then moistened with a solvent (of the binder) to form wet lumps.

Method-II

- ○ Binders are often added in solution form. It requires lower concentration of binder.
- ○ By Method-I the binder is not as effective in reaching and wetting each of the particles within the mass of the powder. Each of the particle in a powder blend has a coating of adsorbed air on its surface, and it is this film of air which must be penetrated before the powder can be wetted by the binder solution.

Method-III

- In direct compression method MCC, microcrystalline dextrose, amylose and PVP are used – those have good flow property and cohesiveness as well.
- It has been postulated that MCC is a special form of cellulose fibril in which individual crystallites are held together largely by hydrogen bonding. The disintegration of tablets containing the cellulose occurs by breaking intercrystallite bonds by the disintegrating medium.

Starch paste

Corn starch is often used in the concentration of 10–20%.

<u>Method of preparation:-</u> Corn starch is dispersed in cold purified water to make a 5 to 10% w/w suspension and then warming in water both with continuous stirring until a translucent paste is formed.. (Actually hydrolysis of starch takes place.)

Liquid glucose:- 50% solution in water is fairly common binding agent.

Sucrose solution:- 50% to 74% sugar solution is used as binder. They produce hard but brittle granules. Their cost is low.

Gelatin solution

- Concentration 10–20% aqueous solution
- Should be prepared freshly and added in warm condition other wise it will become solid.

<u>Method of preparation</u>

- ○ The gelatin is dispersed in cold water and allowed to stand until hydrated. The hydrated mass is warmed in water bath to dissolve.

Cellulosic solutions

HPMC (Hydroxy propyl methyl cellulose) Soluble in cold water.
<u>Method of preparation:</u>

- HPMC is dispersed in hot water, under agitation. The mixture is cooled as quickly as possible and as low as possible
- HEC (Hydroxy ethyl cellulose), HPC (Hydroxy propyl cellulose) are other successful binders
- PVP (Polyvinylpyrollidone) Used as an aqueous or alcoholic solution. Concentration 2% and may vary.

3. Disintegrants

Definition:- A disintegrant is a substance to a mixture of substances, added to tablet to facilitate its breakup or disintegration after administration in the GIT. The active ingredients must be released from the tablet matrix as efficiently as possible to allow for its rapid dissolution.

Disintegrants can be classified chemically as: Starches, clays, celluloses, alginates, gums and cross-linked polymers.
Starch

- Corn starch, potato starch.
- For their disintegrating effect starches are added to the powder blends in dry state.

Mode of action:

- Starch has a great affinity for water and swells when moistened, thus facilitating the rupture of the tablet matrix.
- Others have suggested that the spherical shape of the starch grains increases the porosity of the tablet, thus promoting capillary action.
- Normally 5% w/w is suggested and for rapid disintegration 10 – 15% w/w may be taken.

Superdisintegrants

Super disintegrants like Croscarmelose - cross linked cellulose, Crospovidone - cross linked polyvinyl pyrrolidone and Sodium starch glycolate- cross linked starch

Mode of action

- Croscarmelose swells 4 to 8 fold in less than 10 seconds
- Crospovidone acts by wicking or capillary action.

- Sodium starch glycolate swells 7 to 12 folds in less than 30 seconds.

Other materials

- ○ Methyl cellulose, Agar, Bentonite, Cellulose, Alginic acid, Guargum, and Carboxymethyl cellulose.
- ○ Sodium lauryl sulfate is a surfactant. It increases the rate of wetting of the tablet, thus decreases the disintegrating time.

4. Lubricant and Glidants Objectives:

- Prevents adhesion of the tablet material to the surface of dies and punches.
- Reduce inter-particular friction, improve the rate of flow of tablet granulation.
- Facilitate ejection of the tablets from the die cavity.

Lubricants are intended to prevent adhesion of the tablet materials to the surface of dies and punches, reduce inter particle friction and may improve the rate of flow of the tablet granulation.

Example: Stearic acid, Stearic acid salt - Stearic acid, Magnesium stearate, Talc, PEG (Polyethylene glycols), Surfactants.

Glidants are intended to promote flow of granules or powder material by reducing the friction between the particles.

Example: Corn Starch – 5-10% conc., Talc-5% conc., Silica derivative - Colloidal silicas such as Cab-O- Sil, Syloid, Aerosil in 0.25-3% conc.

Antiadherents are used for the purpose of reducing the sticking or adhesion of any of the tablet ingredients or powder to the faces of the punches or to the die wall.

5.Coloring agents

Objectives of using colors that (i) It makes the tablet more esthetic in appearance and (ii) Colour helps the manufacturer to identify the product during its preparation. Colorants are obtained in two forms dyes and lakes.

Dyes are dissolved in the binding solution prior to the granulating process. However, during drying their color may migrate to the surface and may produce mottling of the tablet. So another approach is to adsorb the dye on starch or calcium sulfate from its aqueous solution; the resultant powder is dried and blended with other ingredients.

Color lakes are dyes which are adsorbed onto a hydrous oxide of a heavy metal (like aluminium) resulting in an insoluble form of the dye.

6. Flavours and Sweeteners

Flavours are usually limited to chewable tablets or other tablets intended to dissolve in the mouth. Flavor oils are added to tablet granulations in solvents, are dispersed on clays and other adsorbents or are emulsified in aqueous granulating agents (i.e. binder).

The use of <u>sweeteners</u> is primarily limited to chewable tablets. E.g. Sugar

- ◦ **Mannitol**– 72% as sweet as sugar, cooling & mouth filling effect

- **Saccharin**– Artificial sweetener, 500 times sweeter than sucrose

Disadvantages (i) it has a bitter after taste and (ii) carcinogenic

- **Cyclamate**– either alone or with saccharin– it is banned
- **Aspartame (Searle)** – widely replacing saccharin

Disadvantage – lack of stability in presence of moisture

CHAPTER FOUR

MANUFACTURING OF TABLETS

Manufacture of tablets involves certain well defined *steps*: namely:-

i. Pulverization and mixing.
v. Granulation.
v. Compression.
v. Coating (if required)

Pulverization and mixing-

- In this step the different solid / powder ingredients are reduced to the same particle size since particles of different sizes will segregate while mixing.
- Various equipments like Cutter mill, Hammer mill, Roller mill and Fluid energy mill is required to reduce the large lumps.

Granulation Technology-

Granulation: It is the process in which primary powder particles are made to adhere to form large multi-particle entities.

Range of size: 0.2 mm to 4 mm. (0.2 mm to 0.5 mm)

Objectives:-

- To enhance the flow of powder.
- To produce dust free formulations and produce uniform mixtures.
- To improve compaction characteristics.
- To eliminate poor content uniformity of mix.
- To avoid powder segregation. As Segregation may result in weight variation.

Percolation Segregation:- air void Ex- Tea & Coffee jar.
Trajectory Segregation:- kinetic energy Ex- powder heap

(a) Wet Granulation-

Step-I <u>Milling of the drug and excipients</u>

- Milling of the active ingredients, excipients etc. are milled to obtain a homogeneity in the final granulation.
- If the drug is given in solution then during drying it will come up to the surface. To avoid this problem drug is mixed with other excipients in fine state.

Step-II <u>Weighing</u>

- Weighing should be done in clean area with provision of air flow system.
- In the weighing area all the ingredients must not be brought at a time to avoid cross- contamination.

Step-III <u>Mixing</u>

Commonly used blenders are:

a. Double cone blender
b. V – blender
c. Ribbon blender
d. Planetary mixer

Any one of the blender may be used to mix dry powder mass.

Step-IV <u>Wet Massing</u>

- Wet granulation forms the granules by binding the powders together with an adhesive.
- Binder solutions can be added in two methods:

<u>Method-IMethod-II</u>

Drug + Diluent Drug + Diluent

Dry binder is added Binder Solution is added Blended uniformly

Suitable solvent is added to activate the dry binder. Blended in a Sigma - mixer or Planetary mixer till properly wet mass is formed

Therefore, when

- (i) a small quantity of solvent is permissible, **method-I** is adopted and

- (ii) a large quantity of solvent is required **method-II** is adopted.

However, **method-II will give more cohesiveness** than **method-I** if the amount of binder remains constant.

- If **granulation is over-wetted**, the granules will be hard, requiring considerable pressure to form the tablets, and the resultant tablets may have a mottled appearance.
- If the powder mixture is not wetted sufficiently, the resulting granules will be too soft, breaking down during lubrication and causing difficulty during compression.

Step-V -Wet Screening

Wet screening process involves converting the moist mass into coarse, granular aggregates by passage through a **hand screen** (in small scale production) or, passage through an **oscillatory granulator** of **hammer mill** equipped with

screens having large perforations (# 6 – 8 mesh screen).

Purpose

* Increase particle contact point
* Increase surface area to facilitate drying.

Step-VI Drying

- Drying is usually carried out at **600C.** Depending on the thermolabile nature of the drug the temperature can be optimized.
- Drying is required in all wet granulation procedures to remove the solvent, but is not dried absolutely because it will pose problems later on. Hence, certain amount of moisture (1 – 4 %) is left within the granules – known as the *residual moisture.*

Methods: Drying can be carried out
Tray dryers – it may take 24 hrs of drying
Truck dryers – the whole cabinet can be taken out of the dryer
Fluid-bed dryer – carry out drying in 30 mins.

Step-VII Dry Screening

After drying, the granules are make monosize by passing through **mesh screen.**

For drying granules the screen size to be selected depends on the diameters of the punch. The following sizes are suggested:

<u>Tablet diameter uptoMesh Size</u>
3/16 " # 20
3.5 / 16 – 5/16" # 16
5.5/16 – 6.5/16" # 14
7.0/16 or larger # 12

Step-VIII Lubrication of granules

After dry granulation, fine powder lubricant is added. A 60 or 100 mesh nylon cloth is usually used to screen the lubricant onto the granulation, thus eliminating lumps and increasing its covering capacity.

To maintain uniform granule size, the lubricant is blended very gently using tumbling action.

When powder is too fine, it may not feed into the die uniformly, causing density and weight variations.

As lubricants produce hydrophobic surfaces, overblending prevents intergranule bonding during compression since the lubricant produces hydrophobic surfaces.

(b) Dry Granulation

A dry granulation method is used when (i) the effective dose of a drug is too high for direct compaction and (ii) the drug is sensitive to heat, moisture, or both, so wet granulation cannot be used. e.g. many aspirin and vitamin formulations are prepared for tableting by compression granulation.

<u>Steps of granulations</u>
Milling? Weighing ? Screening ? Blending ? Slugging ? Granulation (Dry) ?
Lubrication Compaction.

<u>Slug</u>:

Slug may described as poorly formed tablets or, may be described as compacted mass of powdered material.

Purpose: To impart cohesiveness to the ingredients, so as to form tablets of desired properties.

Method: It is done either by (i) high capacity heavy duty tablet press

(ii) Chilsonator roller compactor.

Advantages of dry granulation over wet granulation

v. No application of <u>moisture</u> (required in wet granulation) and <u>heat</u> (for drying). So the drugs susceptible to either moisture or heat or both can be made by dry granulation. e.g. <u>calcium lactate</u> cannot be used by wet granulation. (Aspirin, Vitamin C).

v. Dry granulation involves <u>less steps</u> and hence <u>less time</u> is required than that of wet granulation.

v. <u>Less</u> steps requires less <u>working space</u> and <u>energy</u>.

v. Since popularity of wet granulation is more that dry granulation because former will meet all the physical requirement for the compression of good tablets.

Direct Compression Method-

Milling Weighing Sieving Blending Compression

Advantages: (i) It is much more quicker than any of the previous process

ii. Minimum number of steps are required.

- Modified diluents, binders etc. are available in the market which assure spherical shape of the granules to modify flow property. However, they are not used extensively.
- If active medicament is less in amount then there will be no problem but in case of high dose large amount of active ingredient is to be replaced by specially treated vehicles to improve flow property or compressibility.
- These specially treated materials are **costly. Tablet Compression**

It can reduce the volume by apply pressure, particle in die are re-arrange, resulting a closer packing structure and reduce space and at certain lode reduced space and increase inter- particulate friction will prevent farther interparticulate friction.

Elastic deformation:- Either whole or a part can change their shape temporarily.

Plastic deformation:- Change shape permanently.

Particle fragmentation:- Fracture into a number of smaller discrete particles.

Find new position- decrease the volume of powder bed- when force increase new particle again under go deformation-particle particle bonds can formed.

Time of loading:- Deformation of particle are **time independent** process in Elastic & Plastic deformation.

Deformation is **time dependent**, when its behavior is referred to Viscoelastic & Viscous deformation.

Degree of deformation:- Some quantitive chang in shape.

Mode of deformation:- type of shape change. <u>**Basic Component of Compression Machine**</u> **Head**- Contain upper punchs, dies, lower punchs. **Body**- Contain operating machinaries.

Hopper- Holding feeding granules.

Dies- Define size, shape of tablet.

Punches – For compression with in dies.

Cam tracks – Guiding the movement of punches.

Feed frame- Guiding the granules from hopper to dies.

Upper turret- Holds the upper punchs. **Lower turret**- Hold the lower punchs. **Die table**- Contain the dies.

Single station – stamping press Multi- station- Rotary press

TABLET PUNCH MACHINE

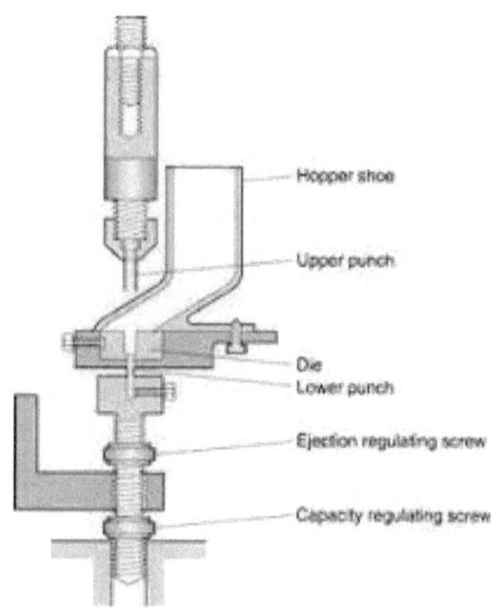

SINGLE PUNCH TABLET MACHINE

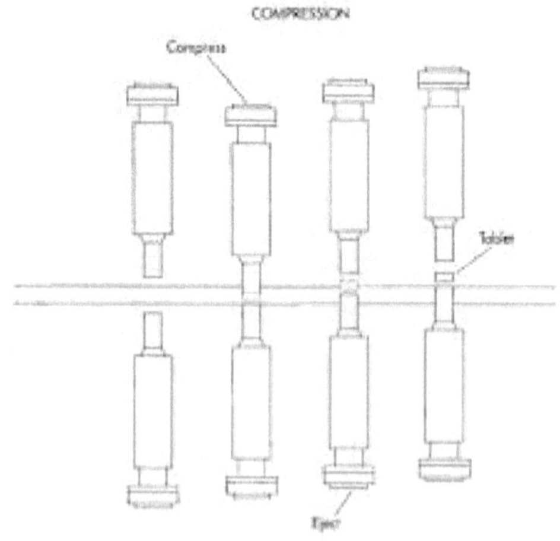

Tablet machine **out put** is regulated by three basic characteristic like:-

- No of tooling sets
- No of compression station
- Rotational speed of press.

Rotary presses are engineered for fast & economical production of all kind of tablet.

Ex- The monestry nova rotary tablet press.

Gradually modification made in machines by using hydraulic or pneumatic pressure to control pressure roll in place of spring for smoother pressure.

Special type machine:-

Fette machine- Chill the compression(For low MP substance like wax)

Versa press- For multi-layer tablet

Tablet Tooling Set

- Its gives definite size, shape of tablet and certain identification marking.
- For this purpose different types of punches are used-
- Flat faced bevel edged.
- Shallow concave (Round / Capsule shaped)
- Standard concave (Round / Capsule shaped)
- Deep concave (Round / Capsule shaped)
- Extra deep.
- Modified ball

Auxillary Equipment-

- Mechanized feeder: Due to short D Well time (Monestry granulation feeding device)
- Mechanized hopper loading equipment:
- Bulk granulation container:
- Electronic monitoring device: To maintain fixed force

CHAPTER FIVE

TABLET PROCESSING PROBLEMS AND SOLUTIONS

An ideal tablet should be free from any visual defect or functional defect. With the development of technology, the production process had become more simplified and more mechanized.

But now the tablet punching machines are all mechanized, the mechanical feeding of feed from the hopper into the die, electronic monitoring of the press, but tablet process problem still persist.

An industrial pharmacist usually encounters number of problems during manufacturing. Majority of visual defects are due to inadequate quality or inadequate moisture in the granules ready for compression or due to faulty machine setting. Functional defects are due to faulty formulation.

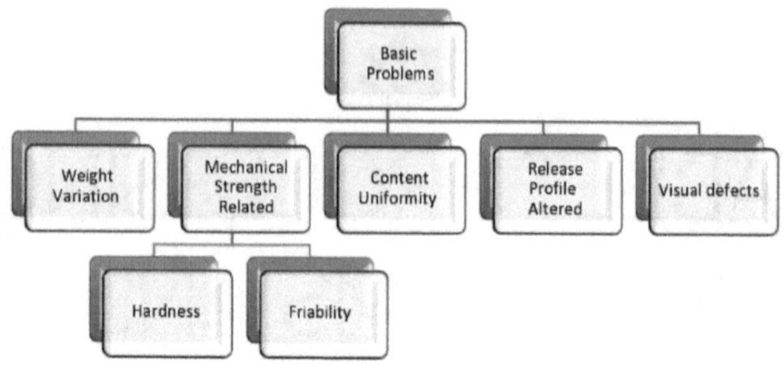

Enter Caption

The **Imperfections** known as: 'VISUAL DEFECTS' are either related to Imperfections in any one or more of the following factors:

I. Formulation design
II. Tableting process

Machine

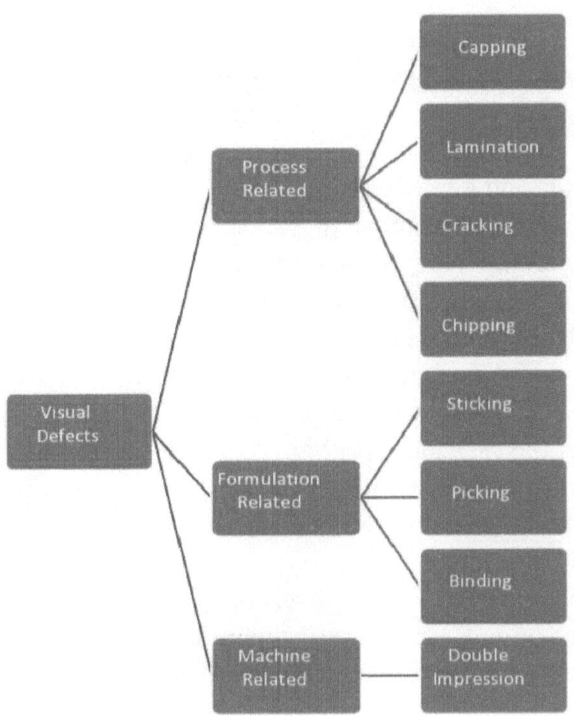

1.Capping and Lamination

Capping is the partial or complete separation of the top or bottom crowns of a tablet from the main body of the tablet.

- **Lamination** is the separation of tablet into two or more distinct layers. Usually these problems are apparent immediately after compression, or even hour or days later.

○ **Detection**: Subjecting tablets to the friability test is the quickest way to reveal such problems.

Reason and Remedies

a. **Reason:** Entrapment of excess air in the granules during compression. If the granules are light and fluffy this type of problems are encountered frequently.

Remedies: Increasing the density of granules by adding more binder or changing the solvent of binder.

b. Reason: New set of punches and dies are very tightly fitted; i.e. the clearance is very negligible hence air cannot come out.

Remedy: In that case punch diameter should be reduced by 0.005" (i.e. 5 thou)

c.Reason: Granules should not be completely dried. if over dried or under dried then capping may take place.

Remedy: So moisture content should be kept within 1 – 4%.

d.Reason: Tooling set used for longer period of time will form claw-shaped curve on tip of the punch or wear ring in die in compression area – this form capping.

Remedy: Punches and dies are changed

2. Picking and Sticking

- **Picking**: -When some portion of the surface of the tablet is removed – it is termed as picking.
- **Sticking:** - Sticking refers to tablet materials adhering to the die wall. Serious sticking at ejection cause chipping.

Causes and Remedies of picking

Cause: When punch tips have engraving or embossing, usually of letters B, A, O are difficult to manufacture cleanly. These may produce picking.

Remedy:

i. Lettering should be designed as large as possible, particularly on punches of small diameter.
ii. Plating of the punch faces with chromium produces smooth, non-adherent face.
iii. Colloidal Silica (Cab-o-sil) is added as polishing agent that makes the punch faces smooth; so that material does not cling to them.

Causes and Remedies of Sticking

Causes: Excessive moisture may be responsible for sticking.

Remedy: Further drying of the granulation is then required.

○ During compression heat is generated and low m.p. lubricants e.g. **stearic acid** may produce sticking.

*Remedy:*Low melting point lubricant are replaced with high melting point lubricants (e.g. **Poly ethylene glycol**)

b. Low m.p. substances, either active ingredients or additives may soften sufficiently form the heat of compression to cause sticking.

Remedies:

- Dilution of active ingredient with additional high m.p. diluents.
- Increase in the size of tablet.
- If a low m.p. medicament is present in high concentration then refrigeration of the granules and then compressing may be the order or using fette compression machine.

3. Mottling

Mottling is an unequal distribution of color on a tablet, with light or dark patches in an otherwise uniform surface.

Cause: Migration of water soluble dyes to the surface while drying.

Remedies:

- Change the solvent system and change the binder system
- Reduce the drying temperature
- Grind to a smaller particle size.
- Use lakes instead of water-soluble dyes.

CHAPTER SIX

EVALUATION OF TABLETS

The compendia, such as the United States Pharmacopeia (USP), and the regulatory bodies, such as the United States Food and Drug Administration (FDA), in addition to historic product-development experience, inform the desired quality attributes of the tablets. Tablets are usually tested for the following characteristics:

Appearance

All tablets should have identical size, shape, thickness, color, and surface markings. The general appearance of the tablet allows monitoring a lot-to-lot and tablet-to-tablet uniformity. Tight control of tablet thickness is required to ensure automated machine operations during its packaging and handling. Tablet-to-tablet thickness within a batch and average thickness of tablets across all batches are defined and controlled.

Uniformity of content

All tablets must be demonstrated to contain the labeled active ingredient and there should be tablet-to-tablet uniformity in drug content. This is usually tested by an analytical method for drug potency (such as high-performance liquid chromatography) in a several individual tablets.

Hardness

Tablet hardness refers to the amount of force required to diametrically crush a tablet. It is representative of the tensile strength of a tablet and is determined by the cohesion characteristics of the powder blend. Tablet hardness impacts tablet disintegration, dissolution, and friability. If tablets are too hard, they may not disintegrate within a reasonable period of time. This can lead to reduced bioavailability and failure to meet the dissolution specification. If they are too soft, then they may not withstand the handling and shipping operations, leading to tablet breakage or chipping (breaking away from edges) and failure during friability testing. Friability is the tendency of the tablets to chip or break by tumbling motion.

Friability

Tablet friability represents the tendency of a tablet to shed powder or break into smaller pieces under mechanical stress, such as falling from a fixed dis-tance. It is a function of the fragility of the compressed powder blend, tab-let shape, cohesion, and hardness. Low tablet friability is desired to ensure its physical integrity during packaging, shipment, and handling.

Weight uniformity

Tablets are compressed at a predefined weight. Under the assumption of normality of statistical distribution of tablet weight, all tablets are required to be within a certain range of the predefined tablet weight. Several tablets are weighed individually, and both the average weight and variation of indi-vidual tablet weight from the average are calculated and controlled during the manufacturing to ensure that the tablets contain the desired amounts of drug substances, with no more than acceptable variation among tablets within a batch.

Disintegration

Disintegration of tablets is evaluated to ensure that the tablet dissolves or breaks apart into smaller particles or granules on contact with water under agitation. This allows the DS to dissolve from its primary particles, being fully available for dissolution and absorption from the GI tract. Tablet dis-integration is evaluated in a standardized apparatus that subjects six tablets to a defined mechanical stress in individual reciprocating cylinders in a suitable aqueous medium at 37°C, to reflect the conditions on oral inges-tion. The time it takes for the last of six tablets to disintegrate into smaller particles and disappear from the reciprocating cylinders is called *disinte-gration time*. The disintegration media required varies depending on thetype of tablets to be tested. The disintegration time is generally not more than 15 min for IR tablets.

The disintegration test is used as a control for tablets intended to be admin-istered by mouth, but not for the tablets intended to be chewable and SR.

Dissolution

As drug absorption and physiological availability depend on having the DS in the dissolved state at the site of absorption, dissolution, also termed drug release, is an important property of tablets. The rate and extent of dissolution of a drug are tested *in vitro* by a suitable dissolution test. Dissolution is used as both a quality control tool to ensure batch-to-batch and tablet-to-tablet uniformity in drug-release characteristics of the tab-lets and sometimes also as a tool for *in vitro–in vivo* correlation (IVIVC) of drug release (*in vitro*) and drug absorption (*in vivo*). Dissolution test provides a means of control in ensuring that a given tablet formulation is similar with respect to the rate and extent of drug release as the batch of tablets were shown initially to be clinically effective.